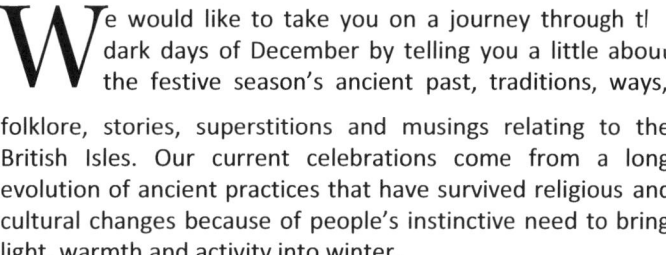

'It was the Yuletide that men call Christmas
though they know in their hearts
it is older than Bethlehem and Babylon,
older than Memphis and mankind.'
H P Lovecraft, 1923

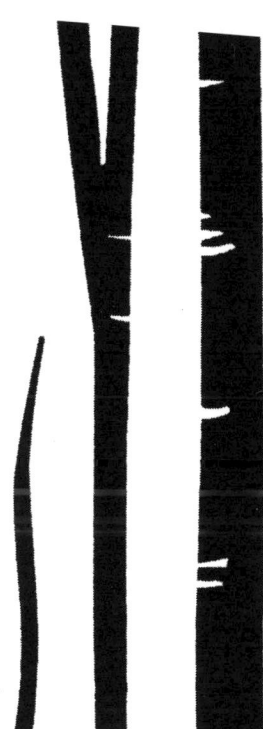

We would like to take you on a journey through the dark days of December by telling you a little about the festive season's ancient past, traditions, ways, folklore, stories, superstitions and musings relating to the British Isles. Our current celebrations come from a long evolution of ancient practices that have survived religious and cultural changes because of people's instinctive need to bring light, warmth and activity into winter.

The page-a-day format aims to give you something to reflect on, do, or find out about, at a relaxed pace whilst helping to keep alive some of the past traditions and their origins. It is of course a mere snippet and our own personal interpretation. Our hope is that it will pique your interest so you will want to find out more about this eclectic mix of celebrations that have a truly complex and cross-cultural identity.

And most of all we also hope you have great pleasure in counting through the days of December and join in with some of the traditions and celebrations still alive today.

Happy Yuletide!

DECEMBER 1
Winter Tales

Winter tales, many of which are passed down through generations, abound with supernatural characters including Father Christmas, magical reindeer, snowmen, Jack Frost, snow and ice queens, elves, angels, fairies, ghosts, ancient deities and Old Father Time.

We think of the long, cold winter nights of yesteryear as having people gathered around fires, telling traditional tales which often turned towards a darker and more fearful side. The idea of seasonal ghost stories was in the psyche of many an author, the best-known probably being Charles Dickens and his story 'A Christmas Carol', in which three spirits visit the main character, Ebenezer Scrooge. Another well-known author, M R James, wrote the following in 1904 as a preface to his first collection, 'Ghost Stories of An Antiquary'; *I wrote these stories at long intervals, and most of them were read to patient friends, usually at the season of Christmas.*

A popular Christmas song, 'The Most Wonderful Time of the Year' even mentions the tradition of telling such tales along with other seasonal activities; *There'll be parties for hosting, Marshmallows for toasting, And carolling out in the snow, There'll be scary ghost stories, And tales of the glories, Of Christmases long, long ago ...*

However it is difficult to know how long this tradition goes back. We know that Yuletide ghost stories were popular in Victorian times because we can still read them but prior to that, they become more difficult to locate. In the 1600s, Shakespeare links the supernatural to winter stories in his play 'A Winter's Tale' when he has the character Prince Mamillius tell the court a story; *A sad tale's best for winter: I have one, of sprites and goblins ...* And of course his play Hamlet is at its essence a winter ghost story. Beginning on a winter's night the opening line of Bernardo, crying; *Who's there?* sets the scene for a wholly disturbing tale.

The playwright Christopher Marlowe, in his play 'The Jew of Malta' (1589), has the character Barabas saying; *Now I remember those old women's words, Who in my wealth would tell me winter's tales, And speak of spirits and ghosts that glide by night.*

More recently in 1950, C S Lewis wrote the magical children's tale, 'The Lion, the Witch and the Wardrobe' which told of an eternal winter brought about by an evil witch and her supernatural minions, where Yuletide celebration and Father Christmas have been banned. Chilling indeed!

We still enjoy the idea of winter stories tapping into the unknown and chilling us in the safety of our own homes. Although winter is no longer the threat it once was to our ancestors, it is still a wonderful time to create and share chilling tales over the long dark nights and keep alive a seemingly long-practised tradition. Perhaps you could have a go?

DECEMBER 2

Orange Pomander

A wonderful way to begin celebrating Yuletide is by making some seasonal decorations. Oranges make the most beautifully-scented natural decorations and have traditionally been used as a base for pomanders since Tudor times. When oranges are dried and placed in a dish with cinnamon stick bundles, fir cones and sprigs of evergreen, you will fill your home with a truly seasonal aroma.

To dry whole oranges, cut a series of five or six vertical slits through the skin, just touching the inner fruit. Then place on a wire rack in an oven set at the lowest temperature. Leave in the oven all day, keeping the door slightly ajar to release the moisture from the oranges. If they are still very moist, you may need to put them in the oven the following day. Finish off the drying process by placing them in an airing cupboard or on top of a warm radiator. When they are ready, the inner flesh will be dry and the slits will have opened up. Rubbing a little gilding paint on the dried skin at this point makes a lovely finishing touch.

To dry orange slices, cut the fruit thinly in horizontal slices and dry in the oven—the same way as whole oranges. Keep checking them as they only take a few hours to dry, then place them on a radiator to finish drying. These slices look wonderful strung together and hung in windows for a stained glass effect, or interspersed with cinnamon sticks, evergreen leaves, star anise and cranberries. Both the whole oranges and the slices can be sprinkled with a spice mix of cinnamon, nutmeg and ginger to give an additional seasonal aroma.

To make orange pomanders you will need 4 oz ground cinnamon, 2 oz ground cloves, ½ oz allspice, ½ oz grated nutmeg, ½ oz ground coriander, 4 oz whole cloves and six oranges (Seville work particularly well). Mix all the spices in a dish large enough to hold your oranges. Using a small skewer or cocktail stick pierce the orange peel and insert whole cloves in the holes, then roll the oranges in the spice mix to coat them. Cover the dish and leave it in a warm place to cure for as long as possible. Turn the pomanders daily. In time, the oranges will dry and take up a wonderful scent of spices. You can fix ribbons around the pomanders to hang them up or place them in a decorative dish. If you are in a hurry, you can part dry the oranges in an oven to begin the drying process.

Keep your orange decorations in an airtight tin and they will last for years, although you can revive them occasionally using sweet orange or bergamot essential oils.

DECEMBER 3

The Cailleach Bheur

In Gallic regions, the Cailleach Bheur was a personification of winter who appeared in the form of an old woman. Her name means 'the veiled one', although she is often referred to as 'the hag', and in some tales she is a giant and coloured blue. This seasonal deity, who rules the winter months between Samhain and Beltane (October 31st to May 1st), is believed to turn to stone on May Day and become human again on All Hallows' Eve. She herds deer, is a guardian to animals during winter, carries a staff that freezes the ground as she walks and battles with the spring in a bid to keep an icy grip on nature for as long as possible. In Scotland, she is also known as Beira, Queen of Winter, and such is her status that she was considered by some to be the mother of all goddesses. She is said to have formed mountains and large hills whilst striding across the land and accidentally dropping rocks from her creel (wicker basket) and that she carried a hammer for shaping hills to use as stepping stones.

In winter she washes her 'great plaid' (giant kilt) in the Gulf of Corryvreckan, on the west coast of Scotland, a place known as the 'Cauldron of the Plaid'. The process takes three days and is so vigorous that it swirls up a tempest and so noisy that it can be heard twenty miles away. By the time she has finished, her plaid is pure white and a blanket of snow covers the land.

On Bridgid's Day (February 1st) the Cailleach gathers her firewood for the rest of the winter. It is said that she makes sure the weather is bright and sunny, so she can gather enough firewood to keep herself warm during a prolonged winter. However, if the weather is foul on Bridgid's Day it is said the Cailleach is asleep and will run out of firewood, meaning winter will soon end.

On the Isle of Man, where she is known as Caillagh ny Groamagh, if people see a large bird carrying sticks on Bridgid's Day, they believe it is Caillagh and a sign that winter will continue a little longer.

In Scotland and Ireland, there is a tradition for the farmer who is the first to bring in his grain harvest to make a corn dolly from the last sheaf gathered. This represents the Cailleach (sometimes called 'the Carlin' or 'Carline' meaning from the last sheaf of the crop). The figure is then thrown into the field of a neighbouring farmer who has not finished harvesting. The last farmer to bring in his crop was responsible for taking the corn dolly in and caring for her until the following harvest time.

DECEMBER 4
Waits & Carolling

Christmas 'waits' came from a long musical tradition associated with the run-up to the festive season. They were groups of singers and musicians who sang and played carols for money around their town or village during the evenings of Yuletide. They probably derived from town 'waites', a position that dated from mediaeval times and were night watchmen who patrolled the streets whilst playing an oboe-like instrument called a 'hautboy'. Their loud, penetrating sound marking the passage of the hours let people know they were on duty. Other instruments were also used, such as the 'shawm', known as the 'wait pipe', bass viol, fiddle and bassoon. Waits received salaries and liveries and wore a silver chain of office bearing the town's Coat of Arms. They were later disbanded following the Municipal Corporations Act of 1835. The surnames Waite and Wakeman are derived from individuals who would have worked as 'waites'.

We traditionally refer to the songs sung throughout Yuletide as carols, a word that probably derives from the old French word 'carole', meaning a circle or round dance accompanied by singers. The first carols were old traditional folk songs which had new words added and accompanied dances.

These songs were sometimes called 'noels', the French word for Christmas. Some carols, such as 'Good King Wenceslas' and 'The Holly and the Ivy', can be traced directly back to the Middle Ages, and are among the oldest musical compositions still sung regularly today. The oldest carol known to have been written on our islands is the Anglo-Norman carol. Dating from the thirteenth century, it tells not only of Christmas celebration and praising God but of bringing people together particularly in verses 1, 3, 4 and 5.

1.
Lordings, listen to our lay—
We have come from far away
To seek Christmas;
In this mansion we are told
He his yearly feast doth hold;
'Tis t-day!
May joy come from God above,
To all those who Christmas love.

3.
Lordings, through our army's
band They say—who spends
with open
  hand
Free and fast,
And oft regals his many friends
—God gives him double what he
  spends
To grace the day.
May joy come from God above,
To all those who Christmas love.

4.
Lordings, wicked men eschew,
In them never shall you view
Aught that's good;
Cowards are the rable rout,
Kick and beat the grumblers
out, To grace the day.
May joy come from God above,
To all those who Christmas love.

5.
To English ale and Gascon wine,
And French, doth Christmas
much
  incline—
And Anjou's, too;
He makes his neighbour freely
drink So that in sleep his head
doth sink Often by day.
May joy come from God above,
To all those who Christmas love.

DECEMBER 5
Seasonal Superstitions

This special time of the year is associated with many superstitions. For example, bad luck was believed to visit those who failed to observe certain customs; such as abstaining from singing carols during months other than December, ceasing to work through the twelve days of Christmas and kissing under the mistletoe. Even opening the door on Christmas morning was the subject of superstition, as the first person to do so should always say 'Welcome Old Father Christmas' to ensure a good year ahead.

Many superstitions arose from concern about certain items leaving the house, particularly fire. This meant that 'borrowing fire', which was the commonplace practice of taking burning embers from a neighbour's fire to start your own, was considered very bad luck on Christmas Eve and Christmas Day. Equally, money, food or candles should not leave the house. Keeping things alight was also a keenly-observed superstition, with the Yule log being kept alight for the twelve days; candles remaining alight all night on Christmas Eve (and in some cases throughout Christmas Day) and candles kept burning in a window to console the lonely traveller.

To bring good luck, eating twelve mince pies from twelve separate friends during the twelve days of Christmas would ensure twelve months of good fortune (and feeling very full!). In addition, the Christmas pudding should be stirred by all in the household whilst it is being made, traditionally on Stir Up Sunday (the Sunday before Advent); some say you should stir it three times clockwise and then make a wish. Charms, such as a silver sixpence, are added to the pudding mix, bringing good luck to all who find one when eating the pudding.

Using greenery to decorate the home had its own rules too. If ivy was used alone, or if there was more ivy than holly, it was considered a bad omen. Decorations should not be put up before Christmas Eve and must be taken down by Twelfth Night to avoid bad luck. Until the nineteenth century there was a general consensus that evergreen decorations should be burned after they were taken down. Although, it was later considered back luck to do so. At one time it was believed that decorations should remain up until Candlemas (February 2nd)!

Christmas Day was thought to be the luckiest of days to be born and anyone born on that day would never suffer the fate of hanging or drowning, or be troubled by ghosts and spirits. For those who 'pass' at Christmas, it was believed in Ireland that the gates of Heaven opened at midnight on Christmas Eve to let their souls straight through. And if we happen to have snow at Christmas we at least know it will mean Easter will be green!

DECEMBER 6
Who is Father Christmas?

The idea that we are visited on Christmas Eve by an old man who flies through the sky in a sleigh pulled by magical reindeer, and who is assisted by elves, does not trouble us at all. In fact, this story has been passed down the generations with our own children encouraged to be a part of this folklore. It is probably one of the last stories in our culture that we all share excluding religious stories.

But why does this story exist? If we ignore the recent commercialisation of Father Christmas, particularly associated with his guise as Santa Claus, we can see a longer history that taps into the customs and beliefs of different nations. He is known by many different names and guises (not always human). In Scandinavian regions, the Jullboc is a goat who played tricks on people and also gave gifts. The Finnish word for Santa Claus, Joulupukki, literally means Yule Goat. Nisse (Danish and Norwegian), Tonttu (Finnish) and Tomte (Swedish) all refer to a small bearded old man, a 'gnome-like creature' who is both mischievous and helpful and who expects a bowl of porridge, topped with a pat of butter on Christmas night. At some time in the 1840s, the Danish Nisse turned into a Julenisse (Christmas Nisse), the bringer of Christmas presents in Scandinavian countries.

Not all stories associated with visitations, gift giving, rewarding good behaviour and punishing bad behaviour are so light-hearted. In Iceland, the Jólasveinar were the thirteen sons of the trolls Gryla and Leppaludi. By all accounts these were frightening creatures who arrived thirteen days prior to Christmas, one by one, and did their utmost to upset the Christmas preparations. A law was issued in 1746 to put a stop to the tales that were frightening children and now the Jólasveinar have grown much milder; children happily put out their shoes on their windowsills to have them filled with gifts.

But the origin of these supernatural visitors is difficult to ascertain. The Norse god, Odin, on his eight-legged horse, Sleipner, who gallops through the sky with his long blond beard flying behind him, punishing the bad and rewarding the good, bears an uncanny similarity to today's Father Christmas riding behind his reindeer. Or perhaps it is from the Roman festivities of Saturnalia that our customs are derived. We do know that, throughout the British Isles, there has been celebration of Midwinter in some form in Gallic, Celtic and Druidic realms.

The tradition of magical beings originating from the fey realm, who are out and about during winter, some being gift givers, many having a potential to cause a bit of mischief that can be placated with food, extends throughout the Yuletide season. We may never know who Father Christmas really is, but we do know that he provides a chance for a bit of magic to enter our lives during the Yuletide season.

DECEMBER 7
Holly (Ilex) &
Ivy (Hedera helix)

Holly and ivy have long associations with each other and are often used together for winter decorations. As both are evergreen, they provide colour in an otherwise drab season. They were also believed to provide protection against evil spirits that roamed abroad during the dark months.

The original words of the ancient carol 'The Holly and the Ivy' were believed to have told of the rivalry between these two evergreens. Other folk songs and verses also recounted this rivalry, such as this one from the fifteenth century;

Holly and ivy made a great party
Who should have the mastery
In landes where they go.

Then spoke holly 'I am free and jolly,
I will have the mastery
In landes where we go'.

Then spake ivy, 'I am lov'd and prov'd,
And I will have the mastery
In landes where we go'.

Then spake holly, and set him down on his knee,
'I pray thee gentle ivy, Say me no villainy,
In landes where we go'.

Superstitions surrounding holly and ivy were especially prevalent around Christmas time and the New Year, and whichever was brought into the house first would dictate whether the master or the mistress ruled the household for the coming year (smooth-leaved holly was believed male, whilst prickly-leaved holly bearing bright red berries was believed to be female).

Christian symbolism connected the prickly leaves of the holly with the crown of thorns worn by Jesus, and the drops of blood he shed with the berries. It was also believed to signify everlasting life, all of which made it a firm favourite to bring in to the church during the Christmas period.

In pre-Victorian times 'Christmas trees' would most likely have been holly bushes planted outside the house as a protection from malevolent faeries. Sprigs of holly within the home were believed to provide a place for faeries to hide so they could avoid encounters with people.

One of the best reasons for growing holly and ivy in your garden is the benefit they provide to wildlife; holly berries provide an essential source of winter food for many birds. Song thrushes, mistle thrushes, blackbirds, fieldfares and redwings feast on them after a frost, which makes them softer and more palatable. They are also a vital food source for the lovely Holly Blue butterfly. Ivy provides nourishment for over one hundred inverte-brates, especially for moths such as the Dotted Chestnut and the Herald, while its flowers are a source of nectar for many species including bees.

DECEMBER 8
Making an
Evergreen Wreath

Making a wreath is a wonderful way to uphold the tradition of using evergreens to adorn the home, as a reminder of life and growth, during the barren months of winter. It also provides a good reason to go out on a winter walk and gather natural materials and greenery, as well as decorative elements such as rosehips, seed heads and berries you can also use moss raked from your garden.

The word 'wreath' comes from the Old English word 'writhen', which means to writhe or twist, and its circular shape symbolizes continuation and the cycle of seasons. To make a wreath base which is wholly bio-degradable, fashion a hoop from flexible stems such as willow, dogwood or hazel. Simply twist the sticks and encourage them into a hoop shape, using jute to tie things in place. The more sticks you use the thicker your wreath and the easier it is to attach things, although some people like to keep it simple and dainty. If you prefer you can buy an 8 to 10 inch metal wreath ring, which has the added advantage of being reusable year on year.

Once you have a circular base, if you have access to moss you can pad the ring with it by making thick sausage shapes and binding them to the ring with jute.

The moss gives you something to push the greenery and dried materials through. If you do not attach moss you will need to bind everything you have gathered to the base using jute.

It is best to attach a base of greenery first, all the way round. Fir, yew or small leafed foliage, such as box or hebe, is quite good for this although some people like to use a larger leaf, such as laurel, to provide a smoother look. For a second layer you can add sprigs of holly, ivy berry heads and any other decorative foliage you have picked. The final layer is where you put the most decorative things you have collected, such as dried seed heads, rose hips, and cones, so they are prominent. You may need to use florist stub wire for this, particularly to attach cones. Other nice decorative items to use are dried orange slices, cranberries threaded on a string or wire, cinnamon sticks and variegated ivy either wrapped around or allowed to trail.

Check as you attach things that they are secure by giving the wreath a shake; as if it is attached to your front door it will need to withstand quite a bit of movement. For a final flourish add a bow of decorative ribbon, jute or sisal. A sprinkle of seasonal oils such as cinnamon, orange or clove will create a wonderful aroma as people cross your threshold.

DECEMBER 9

Ancient Monuments & Manuscripts

The exact date of the Solstice or Midwinter was not known in ancient times. The literal translation of Solstice means 'the sun stands still' and describes the fact that for a few days that is exactly what appears to happen to the length of day and night. Pliny the Elder suggests it to be December 26th, whilst Bede referred to the English celebrating Modranicht (Mother Night), 'their most important of festivals', on December 24th. He tells us this was considered to be New Year and that a vigil was kept throughout the night, with religious rites taking place. However, it is now thought Bede is referring to an established Anglo-Saxon Christian feast of the Nativity and that the term 'mother' related to Mary, the mother of Jesus. The Nativity festival was simply known as Midwinter by the Anglo-Saxons.

The scribe, Syrus, commented in the margins of a manuscript by the twelfth century Bishop of Amida, Dionysius Bar Salibi, that the church had exploited an existing solar festival when changing the date for celebrating Christmas; *It was a custom of the pagans to celebrate on the same December 25 the birthday of the sun, at which they kindled lights in token of festivity. In these Solemnities the Christians took part. Accordingly, when the church authorities perceived that the Christians had a leaning to this festival, they took counsel and resolved that the true Nativity should be solemnized on that day.*

There has long been a belief that proof of an ancient celebration of the Winter Solstice lies in the remains of the monuments scattered across our isles. People have debated whether they were deliberately built in an alignment that marked the path of the sun, therefore showing reverence to our life-giving star. Notably, the most famous of ancient monuments, Stonehenge, which has in recent times been a focal point during the Summer Solstice, is considered by some to have been built to mark the Winter Solstice. More recent evidence relating to Stonehenge suggests that the tallest stone points towards the sunrise on the Midwinter Solstice; a new alignment at 80 degrees to the line of the axis of the monument, has been discovered that points to Midsummer Solstice sunrise and Midwinter sunset.

There is good evidence that people gathered at ancient sites during winter at two megalithic monuments; Newgrange in County Meath, Ireland, and Maeshowe on Orkney, Scotland, both of which demonstrate a solar alignment to the Winter Solstice sunrise. Archaeological evidence at these sites confirms that they were occupied during the winter months of December and January and indicates, by the sheer number of animal bones found, that a good many people must have gathered there. Perhaps you could visit an ancient site to mark the Solstice, which falls on either December 21st or 22nd.

DECEMBER 10

Parlour Games

Entertainment has always been an important part of the Yuletide holidays. If you were not out visiting or being visited, dancing, singing, taking part in sports, storytelling, playing cards, strolling or watching travelling entertainers, you may well have been playing what became known as parlour games. By today's standards many of the games people played would have been banned under the Health and Safety Act.

One such game was Snap-dragon (also known as Flap-dragon), believed to have been played as early as the sixteenth century. Brandy would be heated and set alight in a wide, shallow bowl containing raisins. The aim of the game was to pluck the raisins out of the burning brandy and eat them. It was described in Samuel Johnson's Dictionary of the English Language, 1755, *as play in which they catch raisins out of burning brandy and extinguish them by closing the mouth and eating them.* It became firmly established when it was mentioned in 'The Pickwick Papers' by Charles Dickens, in 1836, and in Anthony Trollope's 'Orley Farm', in 1861. In 'Through the Looking-Glass and What Alice Found There' written in 1871, Lewis Carroll describes; *A snap-dragon-fly. Its body is made of plum pudding, its wings of holly-leaves, and its head is a raisin burning in brandy.* Robert Chambers' 'Book of Days', in 1879, mentions that the game was accompanied by a chant;

Here he comes with flaming bowl,
Don't he mean to take his toll,
Snip! Snap! Dragon!
Take care you don't take too much,
Be not greedy in your clutch,
Snip! Snap! Dragon!
With his blue and lapping tongue
Many of you will be stung,
Snip! Snap! Dragon!
For he snaps at all that comes
Snatching at his feast of plums,
Snip! Snap! Dragon!
But Old Christmas makes him come,
Though he looks so fee! fa! fum!
Snip! Snap! Dragon!
Don't 'ee fear him but be bold —
Out he goes his flames are cold,
Snip! Snap! Dragon!

Another popular game was Blind Man's Bluff (or Buff as it was originally known). The principle was that one player, known as 'It' was blindfolded, spun round to disorientate them and then asked to search for the other players to tag or identify. The other players were allowed to put them off by shouting or by giving them a 'buff', a supposedly gentle nudge to put them off track. The game ends when all are tagged, then either the first or last correctly identified person becomes 'It' for the next game.

Word games such as 'How? What? Where? When?' and 'The Minister's Cat' were also enjoyed, together with dice, cards, charades and magic tricks. Perhaps this year you could make your own fun and play traditional games with friends and family and recapture the fun of yesteryear.

DECEMBER 11
Welsh Celebrations

Yuletide in Wales known as, 'y gwyliau', meaning 'the holidays', were marked by a succession of activities which took place over the twelve-day Christmas period. A carol service, known as the 'plygain', was traditionally held between the hours of three and six on Christmas morning. Activities such as singing, dancing and toffee-making would take place during the night to keep people awake and occupied until it was time to leave for church. The villagers would process to the church carrying candles and torches. The candlelit church was thought to symbolize the coming of 'The Light of the World'. The rest of Christmas Day was devoted to eating, drinking and revelry, with sports and games taking place during the afternoon.

Other activities taking place during the festive period included the Mari Lwyd horse ritual, which was performed by men and boys in South Wales. The Mari Lwyd (Grey Mare or Holy Mary) was a horse-skull figure who was carried from door to door by a wassail-singing group. The Mari Lwyd and his attendant and singers began the ritual by singing traditional stanzas at someone's front door whilst trying to gain entry. This would take the form of a challenge to an opponent inside the house, called the 'pwnco'. He would then sing back to the group and rivalry and leg-pulling would take place. If victorious, the Mari Lwyd would enter the house for ale and cakes (and sometimes money). The group would then sing additional stanzas to introduce its individual members and entertain the occupants of the house, and finally, a farewell song.

Giving gifts of bread and cheese on New Year's Day is an old custom in Wales. Children went from house to house collecting New Year's gifts including 'callenig' which was an apple supported on a tripod of twigs and studded with straw and cloves, with a sprig of box or other evergreen inserted at the top. There are accounts of them being smeared with flour, stuck with nuts, groats or wheat berries and topped with thyme or other fragrant herbs.

In English, the word 'calennig' can be translated as the 'first day of the month'. Quite what its purpose was is unclear, but some think the custom dates back to pagan times. The calennig was not thrown away but was kept in a window, bringing good luck for as long as it stood there. This verse is associated with calennig and was recited at the door;

Mi godais heddiw ma's o'm tŷ   *(I left my house today)*
A'm cwd a'm pastwn gyda mi,   *(With mybag and my stick)*
A dyma'm neges ar eich traws,   *(And here is my message to you)*
Sef llanw'm cwd â bara a   *(Fill my bag with bread and*
chaws.   *cheese.)*

DECEMBER 12
Frumenty

It is believed that Christmas Pudding as we know it today began life as 'frumenty' or 'furmety'. For centuries, frumenty was part of the traditional Celtic Christmas meal and has been described as England's 'oldest national dish'. Its name is derived from the Latin *'frumentum'*, meaning 'grain'. In Yorkshire, it was 'the first thing eaten on Christmas morning, just as ale posset was the last thing drunk on Christmas Eve'.

During the early nineteenth century it was said that; *'Christmas Eve is celebrated in almost every family by a supper of frumenty, made of steeped wheat boiled with milk, followed by apple pie, cheese and yule-cake'.*

The Chief Master Cook to King Richard II, c.1390, gave the following receipt for making frumente in 'The Forme of Cury';

Tak clene whete & braye yt wel in a morter tyl the holes gon of; seethe it til it breste in water. Nym it up & lat it cole. Tak good broth & swete mylk of kyn [cow] or of almand & tempere it therwith. Nym yelkes of eyren [eggs] rawe & saffroun & cast therto; salt it: lat it naught boyle after the etren ben cast therinne. Messe it forth.

Here is a more modern recipe if you want to try making this seasonal dish. Ingredients: 5 oz cracked bulgur wheat, or pearl barley as an alternative; 1 pint ale; 1 large egg; 2 handfuls of currants or other dried fruit; ½ tsp cinnamon, nutmeg and ginger; 4 tbsps of single cream; water; generous pinch of saffron. Soak the wheat in the ale until it begins to swell; this takes a few hours and most of the liquid should be absorbed. Add the spices then boil for a few minutes until the wheat is soft. If the mixture becomes too dry while it is cooking add extra water. Remove from the heat and add the dried fruit then allow to cool before adding a beaten egg and the cream. Cook on a low heat, but do not allow it to boil, then add the saffron for colour and flavour.

The dish was either served as an accompaniment to meat or as a sweeter recipe on its own—possibly to those of a higher status because of the high value placed on wheat. During the nineteenth century, frumenty was so popular that it was possible to buy the wheat pre-boiled and set into a jelly; this was called 'creed wheat' (to 'cree' grain means to soften it by soaking or boiling).

The Yuletide version had the addition of exotic fruits and spices (if you could afford them) and cream and honey. It was usually soaked in ale, but may also have had a slug of brandy added.

Frumenty could be made with a meat stock, rather than ale or water, to give it a more savoury flavour.

DECEMBER 13

Mischief & Mayhem

Throughout the dark days and nights of Yuletide it was thought that spirits could wander and fey folk were abroad causing mischief. It was believed the powers of darkness held sway, so great fires were lit to keep them at bay. In the Orkney's, 'trows' —malignant, mischievous fey spirits—would leave the underworld to dance in the human world. While in England, Herne the Hunter rode the night sky gathering souls; spirits would congregate at 'places of old magic' whilst devils planted evil deeds into the hearts of people.

During the 'Twelve days of Yule', as the weak sun struggled to gain strength, people were fearful of chaos and misrule: these days were sometimes referred to as the 'days of the unblessed'. In the late mediaeval and early Tudor period, a person of lowly status was appointed as the 'Lord of Misrule'. This tradition appears to have evolved from the times of Roman occupation and their winter festival, Saturnalia. The Lord's role was to manage festivities held at court, in fine houses, in law schools of the Inns of Court, and in many of the colleges at Cambridge and Oxford univer-sities; he also presided over festivities and held mock courts, during which he was paid comic reverence.

His role lasted anything from twelve days of Christmas to three months. John Stow, in his 'Survey of London', published in 1603, gives the following description;

In the feaste of Christmas, there was in the kinges house, wheresoeuer hee was lodged, a Lord of Misrule, or Maister of merry disports, and the like had yee in the house of euery noble man, of honor, or good worshippe, were he spirituall or temporall. Amongst the which the Mayor of London, and eyther of the shiriffes had their seuerall Lordes of Misrule, euer contending without quarrell or offence, who should make the rarest pastimes to delight the Beholders. These Lordes beginning their rule on Alhollon Eue [Halloween], continued the same till the morrow after the Feast of the Purification, commonlie called Candlemas day. In all which space there were fine and subtle disguisinges, Maskes and Mummeries, with playing at Cardes for Counters, Nayles and pointes in euery house, more for pastimes then for gaine.

However many considered the misbehaviour was becoming out of hand. In the 1580s, Philip Stubbes, author of The Anatomie of Abuses, complained;

That more mischief is that time committed than in all the year besides, what masking and mumming, whereby robbery whoredom, murder and what not is committed? What dicing and carding, what eating and drinking, what banqueting and feasting is then used, more than in all the year besides, to the great dishonour of God and impoverishing of the realm.

DECEMBER 14
Mistletoe
(Viscum album)

The origin of this parasitic plant's association with Yuletide is unclear. It may be because it appears at its best during this time of the year, adorned with white berries and is on clear show, due to the absence of leaves on its host plant.

William Stukeley, the eighteenth century antiquarian, who revived an interest in druids, published Pliny the Elder's account of druid priests cutting mistletoe with a golden sickle, from the oak groves which were held sacred by the druids. Pliny believed it to have special powers and must be caught before falling to the ground to retain its magical properties. The harvested plant could then be used for ritual and medicine.

The best-known tradition, kissing under the mistletoe, is thought to be a remnant of an ancient fertility rite associated with the Roman feast, Saturnalia. There are many rules about kissing under the mistletoe, for example it is bad luck to refuse; a kiss can only be given if the plant has berries and a berry must be plucked on each kiss.

Mistletoe is also reputed to ward off evil, particularly in Nordic legends, and in some parts of the British Isles it would be suspended outside houses and barns to keep witches at bay.

Taking down mistletoe and its disposal are also connected with many, often contrary, superstitions. It must be kept hanging for a full twelve months; it is bad luck to keep it in a home after twelfth night; it must be ceremo-niously burnt, or it should be buried. The church establishment were very suspicious of mistletoe because of its association with magic, pagan beliefs and fertility, so much so that many churches refused to include it in the evergreen decorations adorning the church during the Yuletide season.

The Mistle Thrush, which is larger and paler than the Song Thrush, plays an important role in propagating mistletoe. The berries are eaten by the thrush, which digests the flesh and then excretes the sticky seeds, which will germinate if left on a suitable location. The Mistle Thrush has several other names including *stormcock* due to the male having a loud, far-carrying song which can be heard even during stormy weather; and *holm thrush*, *hollin cock* or *holm cock* which refer to its habit of eating holly berries ('holm' being an old name for holly). Sadly these birds are not as commonplace as they once were due to changes in farming practices, so having trees and bushes with berries in your garden and if you are lucky, even some mistletoe, will encourage and help them.

DECEMBER 15
Strength in the Face of Adversity

During the winter of 1865, Reverend E Donald Carr, the Rector of two parishes in the Shropshire hills, made a journey through the worst snowfall for over fifty years.

Having completed the morning service at Woolstaston Church, he set off on horseback towards Rattlinghope, around four miles away, accompanied by his servant. He soon ran into snow drifts, making the track quite impassable, so he sent the servant back with the horses and continued on foot along a route that he knew well and arrived in time for the service. Afterwards, ignoring the pleas of the parishioners to stay overnight, he started back. However, the snow was soon thigh deep and he was forced to make his way on his hands and knees. The glare from the snow disori-entated him and the icy wind was so painful that he could not look up. He was knocked from his feet and blown over the edge of a slope, yet he had the presence of mind to curl himself into a ball and dig his heels into the snow to stop his fall, which could have ended on the rocks that he knew lay below. He found himself hanging over the edge of a crag and had to pull himself back up and then crawl down the hill.

It was here that he encountered a twenty-foot snowdrift which he had to dig his way through. He was now completely lost and night was beginning to fall. Knowing that stopping would mean certain death, he continued walking, crawling and falling through the freezing landscape. Even the coming dawn brought little relief as a heavy fog clung to the hills, preventing him from recognising where he might be. By now he was snow blind and suffering from frostbite. Mercifully, he could still hear and eventually became aware of the sound of running water, which he tried to follow, hoping it would lead him downhill. Just in time, he noticed a difference in the sound and managed to stop himself falling over the edge of a waterfall. In the deep snow he lost both boots, which were drenched and stretched. Exhausted, he knew he was close to the end and began to make his peace with God.

Suddenly, he heard the sound of children and called out to them for help. On recognising him, they helped him to a cottage where he was tended by a doctor, then taken home. After a long period of convalescence he made a full recovery and wrote an account of his ordeal, which had lasted twenty-two hours. Only willpower and prayer had kept him fighting for survival during a snowstorm that took many lives.

His lost boots are still on display in the local museum and symbolize his heroic struggle against the elements.

DECEMBER 16

Kissing Bough

The kissing bough was a popular Midwinter decoration in the Middle Ages. It evolved from a circlet of twigs, with spokes across its diameter, into a ball shape, made of five hoops of greenery. In its earliest format it was known simply as a 'bunch' and probably was just that, a gathered bunch of seasonal plants.

In Europe, it was customary to hang a small treetop, upside down, to symbolize the Holy Trinity. This was used as an all-year-round decoration and was believed to bring blessings on any household that had one. It is believed that it was customary to embrace the master and mistress of the house under this decoration as a sign of goodwill when visiting. It is difficult to say if this tradition was followed in British homes as there is no evidence, but the kissing bough appears to have come from this tradition of greenery being used decorating homes and having symbolic meaning.

The hoops of the kissing bough were originally made of twigs bent into shape, but later on they were made from carved wood, which could be used again. The hoops were covered in holly, ivy, rosemary, bay, fir and any other evergreen plants. Inside the hoops red apples were suspended using decorative fabric ribbons, if they could be afforded, which were threaded inside the ball, at the bottom, or around the horizontal hoop. A bunch of mistletoe was sometimes hung from the base of the kissing bough and this is believed to be the first time it was used as a decoration. The design developed to include more elaborate decorative flourishes including nuts, oranges and shiny objects and strips of fabric. Another version of the decoration was known as the crown and consisted of the top half of the globe shape on a flat base hoop.

It is said that in 1563, Queen Elizabeth I gifted a kissing bough to Kenilworth Castle, the home of her favourite, Robert Dudley, the Earl of Leicester. In view of the attachment between the Queen and her Earl it seems a very romantic gesture and perhaps provided a good opportunity to embrace in public.

The Georgians continued the tradition and hung apples from the base of the ball and candles atop. By Victorian times the choice of greenery used depended on the meaning attributed to it, as they had become interested in floriography. Lavender and rosemary signified loyalty and devotion, while thyme promoted courage. Mistletoe was a popular decorative choice, symbolizing good fortune and fertility. The Victorians also firmly established the tradition of a romantic kiss under mistletoe, which was an intrinsic part of the decoration, and probably developed many of the superstitions associated with it.

DECEMBER 17
Mulled Drinks
& Mince Pies

The term 'mulling' originates from the seventeenth century and refers to warming a drink by adding heat and/or spices. This recipe for 'Hypocrace', from The Good Housewives Jewel, by Thomas Dawson, 1596 is one of the earliest records of this type of drink; *Take a gallon of white wine, sugar two pounds, of cinnamon, ginger, long pepper, mace not bruised, galingall [possibly the name for root ginger] and cloves not bruised. You must bruise every kind of spice a little and put them in an earthen pot all day. And then cast them through your bags two times or more as you see cause. And so drink it.*

Often associated with the winter season, mulled drinks were popular as a 'winter warmer' to restore circulation. People traveling in draughty carriages would carry a mulled drink to keep them comfortable on their journey or drink them at hostelries along the way.

This contemporary mulled tipple requires 2 bottles of red wine, ¼ pint of brandy, ¼ pint water (optional), 2 oranges (sliced), 2 sticks of cinnamon, 2 tsp ground nutmeg, 5 cloves and 4 tbsp of honey (or to taste). Add all the ingredients to a large saucepan and slowly heat through (do not boil or heat too quickly as this removes both alcohol and flavour). Stir every now and again to dissolve the honey and disperse the flavours. Keep on a very low heat and serve warm from the saucepan.

Other variations include 'Mulled Bishop' (port wine mulled with oranges and cloves) and 'Mulled Negus' (white wine and hot water with sugar, lemon juice and nutmeg). Cider or ale can replace the wine and brandy or, to make a non-alcoholic mulled drink, replace the alcohol with apple or cranberry juice.

As you drink your mulled wine sitting by the yuletide fire, you may want to raise your cup and recite the Nine Elements Celtic Blessing:

May you go forth under the strength of heaven,
under the light of sun, under the radiance of moon;
May you go forth with the splendour of fire,
with the speed of lightning, with the swiftness of wind;
May you go forth supported by the depth of sea,
by the stability of earth, by the firmness of rock;
May you be surrounded and encircled,
with the protection of the nine elements.

Remember to pour a little from your cup back into the earth in gratitude for what she provides.

And, of course, the perfect accompaniment to this beverage is a mince pie. This fruit-based sweet pie is traceable to the thirteenth century European crusaders who brought back Middle Eastern recipes that contained a mix of meats, fruits and spices. Known by many names, including Shrid Pie and Christmas Pie, it was frowned upon by the puritan authorities, who tried to ban it. Overtime, the recipe gradually evolved to include less meat and more fruits, resulting in the mince pie we know and love today.

DECEMBER 18

Guisers & Mummers

It is often difficult to tell the difference between guisers, mummers and even geese dancers. Guisers were people who wore disguises and were very much associated with Celtic regions, particularly Scotland during Samhain (now Halloween), and probably inspired the trick or treat antics of today. However, such activities were not limited to this particular festival and were also very popular during Yuletide.

Guisers would try to gain entry into people's homes, often singing or dancing and cajoling householders to allow them in for warmth and a treat. In Cornwall, a tradition called geese or goose dancing (which may have been called that because of the local pronunciation of 'guise') was seen in Penzance and St Ives. It usually involved younger members of the community being given licence to behave badly. In 1886, it was reported that the goose dancers were so unruly that people were afraid of them, particularly women, children and the elderly; this led to them being banned in Penzance, although they continued their antics in the winding streets of St Ives. On Shetland, guising took place from Auld Yule Eve and lasted for twenty-four days and nights.

The young people dressed up in straw coats and hats and carried looderhorns, trumpets made from cow horn and, sometimes, an accordion.

Mummers were players who performed traditional plays to all in their neighbourhood (although they might travel up to thirty miles). They would travel to and fro, entertaining people wherever they went in return for money, food and ale. They were often a troop of people who were long-established and used to working together and their costumes and plays were very outlandish. It was said that men could earn more than two weeks' wages in a couple of days by 'mummering'. The players tended to remain in their own locale and local dialects played a large part, as did local news which was incorporated into the play being performed. The mummers have been seen as the forerunners of pantomime but, unlike pantomime performers traditional mummers did not 'ham up' their parts as they often do today. One of the favourite plays involved a hero in combat and usually included a king or St George. There was nearly always an appearance of the devil, a doctor and, often, Old Father Christmas, who may be the presenter of the play (his job was to give the audience any information or background needed to make the play move on). Originally all parts of the play were played by men including the female roles. The origin of 'mummer' is probably a fusion of the Middle French word 'momeur', from the Old French word 'momer', meaning 'to mask oneself', and the Middle English word 'mommen', meaning 'to mutter, or be silent'.

DECEMBER 19
Yuletide

The celebration of Yuletide has become a mix of cultural, religious, historical and commercial ways. The word 'yule' has its origins in the Germanic and Scandinavian languages and the term was also recorded by the Venerable Bede, when referring to the winter months of December and January. The Winter Solstice, Midwinter and Christmas all have a place in Yuletide. The word 'yule' although less frequently used, is still an alternative dialect word in areas where there were Viking settlements, such as Scotland, the Northern regions and the East Midlands.

It was considered important to recognise the shortest day and longest night at the time of the Winter Solstice and to encourage the 'rebirth of the sun' by lighting bonfires to keep evil at bay. Evergreens were cut to represent the survival of life through the harshest of winters and people used them as adornments to decorate themselves, their homes and their animals. Animals were sacrificed, special foods were offered, greetings and good tidings given amongst communities, warming drinks were plentiful and gifts were exchanged. Stories, songs and dance would all have played a part in marking this time of the year, when all around was bleak and barren and there was genuine fear of what was lurking in the dark.

Light and fire became central to the celebration of Yuletide, as many of the ways of the past became incorporated with new meanings. Triumph over darkness was still celebrated, but in the personified form of a saviour who was born during the Yuletide festive season. New interpretations were given to customs which then became traditions for Christians and non-Christians alike. The straw fertility symbols of pagan times became symbols of humility as the baby Jesus began his life impoverished in a stable, the giving of gifts was represented by the Magi bearing gifts and the candle symbolised light and hope.

In rural communities, Midwinter was a time when little labouring was done, due to the harshness of the weather and the shortened daylight hours. In part, this explains the proliferation of saints' feast days, and holy days and the celebration of Advent. The acceptance by the church of many of these long-celebrated customs even went as far as the Feast of Fools and Misrule, probably originating from the Roman festival, Saturnalia, where life became 'topsy-turvy'; boys became bishops and the poor become Lords for a day, or longer.

Sadly, we are losing many of our old ways and customs and, whilst we will make new ones, unlike our past transition from pagan to Christian, when past ways evolved through new interpretations, we now seem unable to give them real meaning in our non-religious, commercial society, where winter no longer has the icy grip it once had during past Yuletide seasons.

DECEMBER 20
Herne the Hunter
& The Great Hunt

Yule was regarded as the season in which supernatural visitations were most common. Stories of a 'wild hunt' can be found in many cultures and, from such folklore, the story of Herne the Hunter and The Great Hunt may have its origin.

Although many places and periods of time have a claim to Herne, it is perhaps the tale originating from the great forest of Windsor during the fourteenth century, in the reign of King Richard II, that is most well-known. Herne was a huntsman and, during a Yuletide hunt for the white stag, he saved the King from being gored by the stag's horns by throwing himself between the animal and the King. He managed to kill the stag but sustained life-threatening injuries. The actions of a wise man named Philip Urswick saved Herne. As part of his treatment Herne had the antlers of the slain deer attached to his head to assist healing.

On returning to health Herne became the King's favourite, but two of the King's huntsmen became so jealous that they sought to besmirch his reputation; they persuaded Urswick that Herne was making fun of his healing abilities and showed no thanks.

As a result, Urswick took his revenge by making it appear that Herne was poaching the King's game. The King dismissed Herne from his post and, in a fit of distress, Herne rode into the forest where he hanged himself from an oak tree.

But the hunters did not celebrate Herne's death for long as they found themselves unable to track deer for the King and, therefore, were useless to the hunt. On seeking Urswick's advice, they confessed their jealous motives to the wise man and were told that they must seek Herne's forgiveness. He summoned Herne's ghost to the oak tree and the men were instructed to begin a hunt that night. But the hunt proved fruitless and the King demanded to know what was going on. The huntsmen then revealed the truth to the King, who felt remorse for his actions towards Herne. One night, King Richard went to the oak and Herne's ghost appeared. He told the King that only the death of the two huntsmen would restore the forest, so King Richard had the men executed.

At midnight on the Winter Solstice, Herne, with an antlered head, returns to ride through the forest and across the night skies. Riding alongside him for eternity are the two resentful huntsmen. Herne and his hounds search for the souls of evildoers, sinners and the damned to join the hunt. It is said they chase the white hart, the harbinger of Herne's downfall. He also appears at the site of the oak when the sovereign is unjust, or close to death, or when the nation is in danger.

DECEMBER 21
Winter Solstice

Note; This page is inter-changeable with the 22nd as the Winter Solstice can fall on either date and in rare occurrences it can fall on the 20th or 23rd

The Winter Solstice is an astronomical phenomenon marking the shortest day and longest night of the year. It has long been held as recognition of rebirth and has been marked by gatherings, rituals and celebrations around that time.

It is often called Yule originating from our mixed ancestry, when our islands were invaded and inhabited by Scandinavian and Germanic peoples, which meant that our culture and folklore became interwoven with traditions that have origins in places other than our homeland. As with all 'conquered' people there comes a point where a melding of traditions and ways takes place and a new interpretation is given to older ways. Dating from the Roman occupation, the midwinter festival of Saturnalia may also have played its part in our celebrations at this time of the year.

Worship of the sun, or at least an interest in the sun, is not unique to our isles. Whether you choose to watch the sunrise or the sunset at the Winter Solstice, you are connecting with the natural world and our greater universe.

Raising our energy and the energy around us at this time can only be a positive thing to do on a cold winter's day or night and perhaps allows us the time to be nostalgic. We can also pay homage to Mother Earth by pouring a little from our cup into the soil as a libation to remind us that we rely on nature and our solar system to survive.

Because there is no recorded ceremony or belief for us to follow on the Solstice we are able to celebrate however we wish. For some, this may mean celebrating the Goddess once again becoming the Great Mother and giving birth to the new Sun King. For others it is the time of the Crone, the Holly Lord, the Oak Lord and Herne the Hunter as escort to the Goddess. It is also seen as a festival of fire bringing light and warmth to the dark cold days of winter. Therefore candles, bonfires and torches often play an important part in people's celebrations.

A wonderful traditional drink, steeped in the history of our isles and our Scandinavian past is mead. Mulled mead is flavoured with spices and oranges or apples and traditionally warmed by plunging a hot poker into it. You could use the Old English/Danish greeting of 'Waes Hael!' meaning 'be well', and the reply 'Drinc Hael!', meaning 'drink and be healthy', as your toast.

DECEMBER 22
Almost Forgotten Seasonal Sayings & Traditions

The Yuletide season is a time of traditions, we do things that are commonplace without thinking about them, such as putting up greenery, eating festive foods, placing a fairy on top of the Christmas tree, and giving gifts. Over the years there have been many traditions and sayings that have got lost in the mists of time. Here are just a few sayings and traditions that are not commonly said or followed now but were once part of the seasonal folklore, many are a bit sombre and so may have been dismissed for that reason in this season of joy.

"He's a fool that marries at Yule for when the bairn's near, the corn's to shear".

"A dirty December, A Christmas to remember".

When the clock strikes Midnight on Christmas Eve, all doors should be thrown open to let out bad spirits. (Midlands) Also in Lancashire, Cheshire & Nottinghamshire, it was believed that bells from buried or flooded villages would chime at midnight and people would go out to such places to hear them.

When the Christmas log is burning take notice of the shadows that are cast by its light on the walls as they may resemble people known to you who will 'pass' during the year ahead. (Wales)

When hanging a stocking at the end of the bed or by the hearth an apple should be placed in the toe for good health and an orange and nut placed in the heel for wealth and good fortune.

The ashes and the charcoal gathered at the end of the twelve days of burning the Yule Log were considered to have magickal properties to cure and protect and were kept and used throughout the year.

The stalks from the last sheaf of corn that had been gathered at harvesttime were saved and made into a 'Dolly', that was hung in the rafters until Solstice or Christmas Day when it was then fed to the cows. The wheat from this sheaf was made into frumenty to be a part of the seasonal meal.

Of course, we can make our own new traditions and have new sayings but it is also good to remember some of the things that have happened before us and keep them alive too.

DECEMBER 23
Yuletide Animals

Many animals are associated with this time of the year—through mention in stories, the use of their images and their involvement in customs and traditions.

The robin is synonymous with Yuletide. It is thought that this jaunty, animated little bird made his way onto cards and gifts in Victorian times, when postmen wore red tunics and were known as 'Robin Redbreasts'.

The wren is also associated with this season—sadly because of the tradition of wren hunting on St Stephen's Day (Boxing Day) when these tiny innocent creatures would be hunted and killed and then tied to the top of an elaborately-decorated pole that was carried to every house in the locality whilst the revellers sang;

The wren, the wren, the king of the birds
St Stephen's Day was killed in the furze
Although he be little, his honour is great
And so good people give us a treat.

At each house, a feather would be plucked and given to each household as a protection against witches. The wren is also associated with ancient druids and was thought to be able to give prophesies.

Cattle were also considered special at this time of year, particularly on Christmas Eve when it was believed they would all kneel in honour of the birth of Jesus and there are stories of all the animals associated with the Nativity being able to speak at midnight. The fifth century Christian poet, Aurelius Prudentius Clemens, is credited with the idea of giving animals human voices at this special time so they could join the angels in adoration on the arrival of the Messiah.

Probably the most magical of creatures associated with Yuletide are the flying reindeer pulling 'Santa's Sleigh'. They were mentioned in Clement Clarke Moore's poem ''Twas Night Before Christmas' (1828). Moore's inspiration for this unusual magical power probably came from his knowledge of the lives and traditions of the Sami tribesmen of northern Scandinavia who fed their reindeer hallucinogenic fly agaric toadstools. The deer's digestive system could remove the poisons from the toadstools while leaving the hallucinogen intact in their urine which the tribesmen would drink causing them to hallucinate and believe their reindeer could fly

However the idea of flying animals pulling sleighs during winter has a long-established tradition in ancient Nordic traditions which is thought filtered into the English tale of Herne the Hunter, wearing a headdress of antlers riding the night sky on a horse-drawn chariot above the great forests of Windsor.

 # DECEMBER 24
Sing-Songs

We all like a good sing-song; it makes us feel happier and lifts the spirits. Yuletide is probably one of the few times in the year when we have the opportunity to sing along with others, and where we know lots of songs off by heart. Whilst many carols have Christian overtones, not all of them started out their lives in this way. 'The Holly and the Ivy' is probably the best example of this as it is known to have ancient origins and existed in many forms.

Many songs known as carols were not religious at all such as 'A Christenmesse Carroll' and 'A Carole in praise of Ale' which is believed to date from the sixteenth century (but possibly earlier) which goes as follows;

A bone, God wot!
Sticks in my throat—Without
I have a draught
Of cornie ale,
Nappy and stale,
My life lies in great waste.
Some ale or beer, Gentle
butler, Some liquor thou us
show, Such as you mash
Our throats to wash,
The best ware that you brew.

Saint, master, and knight, That
Saint Malt hight,
Were pressed between two
stones; That sweet humour
Of his liquor
Would make us sing at once.
Master Wortley, I dare well
say, I tell you as I think,
Would not, I say,
Bid us this day,
But that we should have drink.

His men so tall
Walk up his hall,
With many a comely disk;
Of his good meat I cannot
eat, Without I drink, I wis.
Now give us drink,
And let cat wink,
I tell you all at once,
It sticks so sore,
I may sing no more,
'Till I have drunken once.

'The Twelve Days of Christmas' is believed to have been sung by Catholics during the reformation. Each gift brought by 'my true love' is thought to have a hidden meaning or symbol which relating to Catholicism and was a way for Catholics to proclaim their beliefs in moderate safety. However, some people believe that it was originally a folk song that was given meanings at a later date.

Wassailing and carolling around the neighbourhood, also known as 'luck visits', involved general merry-making, often helped by copious amounts of alcohol. This meant that the general good tidings message of blessings on the house and its inhabitants, which feature in many songs, could get quite bawdy, especially if a gift of food or money was not given. 'The Chuckling Hens' song is a very good example of this, with the refrain;

The cock sat up in the yew tree,
The hens came chuckling by,
I wish the cock would drop a turd
And drop it in your eye.
We wish you Merry Christmas and a Happy New Year.

DECEMBER 25
Wishing You a Very Merry Christmas

One thing is certain—December 25th has been celebrated for a very long time. Our multi-cultural past heritage means this time of the year has a special resonance, whether from our more pagan past, or from the influence of Gaelic, Celtic, Roman, Anglo-Saxon, Norman and other cultures. For centuries people have come together and made merry for many different reasons: the rebirth of the sun, Midwinter, Yule, an agricultural observance or the birth of a Christ child. And yet despite this long heritage we, along with those from our past, are always yearning for something we feel has been forgotten. The poet Robert Southey shared this sense of nostalgia when, in 1807, he wrote the following;

All persons say how differently this season was observed in their father's days, and speak of old ceremonies and festivities as things which are obsolete. The cause is obvious. In large towns the population is continually shifting; a new settler neither continues the customs of his own province in a place where they would be strange, nor adopts those which he finds, because they are strange to him, and thus all local differences are wearing out.

The Christmas we know today, in the main, comes from our Victorian heritage. The Victorians felt that Christmas was not what it once was and decided to do something about it. They had a propensity to amalgamate traditions and customs and were excellent at resurrecting and refining traditions to create an idyll, whilst using new technologies, with an eye on commer-cialism. Charles Dickens, a reformist himself, so brilliantly highlighted a need to show 'goodwill to all men', and reform the conditions and working practices of the poor and needy, in 'A Christmas Carol', as well as describing what is now the model for the perfect Christmas many of us still strive for.

And so we finally arrive at the day itself, after weeks of preparation. What is it we hope for? We want to have a visit from a magical gift-bearing being (provided we have been good!); we may want to attend a religious service; a home decorated by lights, greenery (real or not), and probably a fairy, angel or star (or maybe all three!); to consume a lot of food and drink and to be entertained, and to have time for a nap, or a walk, or both, and we would like to do all this in the warm embrace of our family and friends. All of these customs originate from our past traditions and ways and seem to be inherent within many of us.

Whatever Christmas you achieve, whether it be 'traditional' or a 'new take' on the festive season, may it embrace peace and happiness.

DECEMBER 26
Serenading your Apple Trees

Wassailing derives from a form of salutation known among Saxons and Vikings but, according to some accounts, it dates back to the third century, when Britons had their wassail bowl full of ale, honey, toast and roasted crab apples. Whatever its origins, it developed in apple growing areas as a means of serenading orchards and giving offerings in return for a good harvest.

Wassaile the trees, that they may beare
You many a plum and many a peare;
For more or less fruits they will bring
As you do give them wassailing.

Robert Herrick

The traditional time to wassail trees is Twelfth Night or January 17th, which was old Twelfth Night, although there are accounts of wassailing trees on Boxing Day, Christmas Eve and New Year's Eve. To wassail your own fruit trees, follow this ceremony which was held on Christmas Eve 1853 at an old farmhouse in Hertfordshire and later described in the Illustrated London News; *A bowl of genuine English wassail made of native ale, heightened in flavour with spices, and hissing with a wealth of roasted apples was carried into the orchard by one of the servants of the house in a lantern-lit procession to the best bearing apple tree. With everyone gathered around the tree the servant bearing the wassail bowl sang;*

Here's to thee old apple tree!
Whence they may'st bud, and whence thou may'st blow,
And whence thou may'st bear apples enow!
Hats full! caps full!
Bushel-Bushel sacks full,
And my pockets full too! Huzza!

Then after taking a draught of the wassail from the bowl, he threw the remainder of ale at the tree.

Another ceremony involved a cider-soaked cake being placed on the tree and then guns (charged only with powder) being fired and pots and pans banged to make an unholy racket, while others sang a 'Wassail Song'. This custom was to ward off evil spirits from the orchard and encourage a bountiful crop.

Wassail Recipe
Ingredients: 3 litres of apple juice; 1 litre of ale (can be replaced with cranberry juice); 1 cup of sugar (or less if you can manage); 1 heaped teaspoon of allspice; 2 cinnamon sticks; 1 orange; 30 cloves.

Place all the ingredients, except the orange and the cloves, into a large saucepan. Skewer the orange and insert cloves into the holes and drop it into the pan. Bring to the boil and simmer for at least an hour with the lid on. Allow the liquid to 'sit' for a further three hours and then strain, leaving the sediment behind. The liquid is then ready to be re-heated when needed and a dram of brandy can be added to the glass if a more alcoholic drink is desired. Pour over a slice or two of apple.

DECEMBER 27
Hue & Cry for the Festive Season

When the Puritans 'cancelled' Christmas in the 1650s, Old Father Christmas emerged as a symbol of all that was good about celebrating during the festive period. The hue and cry which followed this decision resulted in a 'pamphlet war', in which his cheery image and voice contrasted sharply with the pious and solemn messages put out by the reformers. Christmas had been a target since the reformation; it was regarded with great suspicion because of what were perceived to be its pagan roots and traditions and leaning towards Catholicism. But even though Christmas was under constant attack, people continued to celebrate it in whatever way they could.

Richard Carpenter, a convert from Catholicism to Protestantism, observed that the recusant gentry were noted for their *'great Christmasses'*. So it is hardly surprising that by the 1640s many English Protestants viewed Christmas festivities as 'the trappings of popery, anti-Christian rags of the Beast'. But despite concerted efforts to abolish Christmas and outlaw the customs associated with it, the people's deep-rooted attachment to midwinter rites could not be overcome.

On 8th June 1647, an 'Ordinance for Abolishing of Festivals' was passed. This stated that Parliament had decreed that feast days, including The Nativity, Easter Sunday and Whit Sunday, would no longer be observed as holy days and, therefore, could no longer be taken as holidays. Five years later people were told markets should be kept open on feast days and there should be no observance of what was commonly called 'Chrystmasse Day'; instead, the second Tuesday of each month should be taken for relaxation to compensate for the loss of holidays.

Opposition was widespread and as well as expressing their objections in pamphlets, people refused to open their shops, and continued to make and eat Christmas pies, even though people were encouraged to *sniff them out* and report them. They even attended services, which were often held in places other than churches. But this behaviour was not without casualties as fighting broke out in many areas between Parliamentarians and Royalists. (It was believed those people who wanted to continue to worship and celebrate were displaying support for the Royalist cause.) Old Father Christmas did eventually triumph when Christmas and all seasonal celebrations were restored with the coronation of Charles II in 1660, together with many other long-held and much-loved traditions, such as maypoles on May Day. We know from Samuel Pepys that *to the joy of many hundred Christians*, the church he attended in London was decorated with rosemary and bays and that he returned home to a Christmas dinner of shoulder of mutton and chicken.

DECEMBER 28
Winter Trees

It is the evergreens which get all the attention during Yuletide, yet winter is the perfect time to see and appreciate the shape and character of our native deciduous trees. All trees wear an overcoat of bark to protect their living wood from the harsh weather, gnawing animals and toxic environmental conditions. Bark has a habit of becoming too tight for the growing tree and different trees deal with this in different ways.

The bark of a weathered oak has a rough, cracked appearance. It keeps its bark throughout its life and just adds new patches as it expands—it evolves from a flexible adolescent into a tall and sturdy grown-up, then finally into a short and stout 'pensioner'. The rough, thick bark encases a strong trunk from which wonderful twisting boughs and zig-zagging twigs spread. It holds its lower limbs almost horizontally, and its ability to hold heavy boughs in that position is sign of its consid-erable strength. There is nothing more magical than seeing the dark silhouette of a mighty oak against a winter starlit sky, as if adorned by twinkling fairy lights in celebration of the Yuletide season.

In contrast, the 'Lady of the Woods', the birch, is full of grace and style, and wears a smooth-to-the-touch, silky, pale coat that it replaces by peeling off its old attire for a fresh and gleaming new look. Unlike its slender silvery trunk, its branches and twigs are bronze in colour and form a lace-like pattern against sunlit winter skies. Usually preferring to stand in an opening a little apart from other trees, the birch deserves to be looked at and admired, especially against a backdrop of dense woodland where it shimmers and sways delicately in a wintery breeze.

In its winter guise, the horse-chestnut allows us to see the unusual wave-like shape of its boughs as it undulates up and down. It carries on its twig tips large sticky baubles, known as 'resting buds', which encase baby leaves curled up and protected against the harshest of elements and ready to burst open in spring.

The tall upright body of the beech, wearing a smooth bark ranging from grey to green, provides a sound of rustling to the scene, whether from the leaves that remain on the younger trees, or those shed on the ground by older trees—as satisfying a sound of paper being ripped off yuletide gifts and scrunched up.

Our deciduous trees form an ever-changing backdrop to our lives and mark the seasonal changes with splendour. Remember to look at them and revel in their presence.

DECEMBER 29
A Time for Reflection

Winter and the Yuletide season appear to attract feelings of nostalgia and remembrance. For many, they can be a time of melancholy and a difficult period to get through, particularly for those who are alone. In this extract from his 1907 poem 'Ballade of Christmas Ghosts', the Scottish poet Andrew Lang, taps into these feelings, remembering those who have left us while telling us a little about Yuletide traditions;

Between the moonlight and the fire
In winter twilights long ago,
What ghosts we raised for your desire,
To make your merry blood run slow!
How old, how grave, how wise we grow!
No Christmas ghost can make us chill,
Save those that troop in mournful row,
The ghosts we all can raise at will!

The beasts can talk in burn and byre
On Christmas Eve, old legends know.
As year by year the years retire,
We men fall silent then I trow,
Such sights hath memory to show,
Such voices from the silence thrill,
Such shapes return with Christmas snow,—
The ghosts we all can raise at will.

These extracts from the 1903 poem, 'Christmas Day in the Workhouse' by George R Sims, highlight the inequality and attitudes which were so rife at a time when people were struggling to bring about social reform;

I came to the parish, craving Bread for a starving wife, Bread for the woman who'd loved me Through fifty years of life; And what do you think they told me, Mocking my awful grief, That 'the House' was open to us, But they wouldn't give 'out relief'.

I slunk to the filthy alley— 'Twas a cold, raw Christmas Eve — And the bakers' shops were open, Tempting a man to thieve; But I clenched my fists together, Holding my head awry, So I came to her empty-handed And mournfully told her why.

I rushed from the room like a madman And flew to the workhouse gate, Crying, 'Food for a dying woman!' And the answer came, 'Too late.' They drove me away with curses; Then I fought with a dog in the street And tore from the mongrel's clutches A crust he was trying to eat.

Yes, there, in a land of plenty, Lay a loving woman dead, Cruelly starved and murdered For a loaf of the parish bread; At yonder gate, last Christmas, I craved for a human life, You, who would feed us paupers, What of my murdered wife!

There, get ye gone to your dinners, Don't mind me in the least, Think of the happy paupers Eating your Christmas feast; And when you recount their blessings In your smug parochial way, Say what you did for me, too, Only last Christmas Day.

DECEMBER 30
Gawain &
The Green Knight

On New Year's Day, King Arthur and his knights were enjoying the revelries of the Yuletide season when, suddenly, the doors of the court were thrown open and a gigantic green figure on a green horse entered the hall. The stranger issued a challenge that one of the court must strike him with an axe on condition that he would return the blow in a year and a day. Arthur accepted the challenge, but Gawain, the youngest of Arthur's knights, begged for the honour in place of his King. The Green Knight yielded his bared neck to Gawain who beheaded him in a single swipe, but the Knight did not fall; instead he picked up his severed head and remounted. Then, holding his bleeding head aloft, he repeated the terms of the pact before whirling his horse around and galloping away.

The following year, Gawain set out to seek the Green Knight. He arrived at the castle of Lord Bertilak de Hautdesert and told him of his quest. Bertilak told him he was very close and persuaded him to rest before continuing. The following day, Bertilak went hunting and told Gawain that he would give him whatever prey he killed if Gawain returned the favour by giving him whatever he gained during the day. As soon as the Lord left, his Lady found Gawain and tried to seduce him, but he did not yield except for a single kiss. When Bertilak returned he offered Gawain a deer and in return received a kiss. The following day, the Lady tried again and again Gawain refused her advances; this time two kisses were offered in exchange for a wild boar. On the third day, she offered Gawain a golden ring, which he refused, so she offered him her girdle of green and gold silk, which was charmed and could protect its wearer from physical harm. Tempted, Gawain accepted. That evening, Bertilak returned with a fox, which he exchanged for three kisses while Gawain kept the girdle a secret.

On the appointed day, with the girdle wound twice about his waist, Gawain set out to meet the Green Knight. Gawain offered his neck to the Knight to receive the fatal blow. At the first swing Gawain flinched and the Knight mocked him. Ashamed of his cowardly act, the second time Gawain did not flinch; but the Knight withheld the blow saying that he was testing Gawain's nerve. Angry, Gawain told him to deliver the deadly blow. This time, the Knight's axe struck home but only delivered a flesh wound because of the protective girdle. Gawain confessed his deception to the Green Knight who told him he was the most blameless knight in all the land and revealed himself to be Bertilak—he had been transformed by the sorceress Morgan le Fay, Arthur's sister. From then on Gawain wore the girdle as a penance and as a reminder to always be honest.

DECEMBER 31

New Year's Eve

The passing of the old year and coming of the new have a significance which encourages many to resolve to change their ways for the better; so many view the last day of the year as the last day of their old ways. Taking time to review the past year is a good way of keeping the vigil until the clocks strike midnight. There is a saying that however you spend the first moments of the new year will indicate how you will spend the rest of the year; so many people feared that sleeping through this period of time would mean being bedridden, plagued by ill health or even death.

The passing of time is symbolized by the sickle-bearing figure of 'Old Father Time' who bids farewell as the New Year arrives, often symbolized as a cherub-like babe. Bells ringing in the New Year remind us that time has passed and we must continue to move forward.

Tennyson's poem, 'In Memoriam', written in 1850 includes the following verse;

Ring out, wild bells, to the wild sky,
The flying cloud, the frosty light;
The year is dying in the night,
Ring out, wild bells, and let him die.
Ring out the old, ring in the new,
Ring happy bells across the snow;

The year is going, let him go,
Ring out the false, ring in the true.

Due to the separate paths taken by the Scottish and English churches at the seventeenth century reformation, New Year's Eve and New Year's Day, known as Hogmanay, became much more celebrated in Scotland and the northern border counties, whilst Christmas Day was the more celebrated in England.

In the past, Twelfth Night marked the end of the Yuletide festivities whereas New Year's Day has now taken on this role; so it is perhaps because of this that New Year has now become more celebrated. In late Victorian times people had already begun to embrace New Year as an opportunity for festivity, with the public often gathering around churches to hear the New Year rung in, taking part in organised singing and exchanging greetings cards and small gifts.

'First Footing' spanned the final moments of the old year and the beginning of the new, with people symbol-ically walking the old year out of their homes after bringing in the new year through the front door. There are many variations of this tradition and people got very confused about the order in which these duties should be carried out, and by whom. This old Nottinghamshire rhyme at least helps with the order;

Take out, take in,
Bad luck is sure to begin
Take in and take out
Good luck will come about.

Printed in Dunstable, United Kingdom

72088957R00020